IMAGES
of America

MICHOUD
ASSEMBLY FACILITY

In 1912, a lone horse-drawn buggy makes it way down a dirt road. At right are the remains of the smokestacks used in the sugar refinery process at the Michoud Plantation, now slowly being consumed by overgrown vegetation. (Courtesy of NASA.)

ON THE COVER: Shown on September 8, 1965, in the assembly stage are three of the twelve Saturn IB booster rockets being built by the Chrysler Corporation. After assembly, the completed boosters were shipped by barge to the George C. Marshall Space Flight Center in Huntsville, Alabama, for static testing and then to Kennedy Space Center (KSC) in Cape Canaveral, Florida, for launch. (Courtesy of the National Archives.)

IMAGES
of America

MICHOUD
ASSEMBLY FACILITY

Cindy Donze Manto

ARCADIA
PUBLISHING

Published by Arcadia Publishing
Charleston, South Carolina

Library of Congress Control Number: 2014944611

For all general information, please contact Arcadia Publishing:
Telephone 843-853-2070
Fax 843-853-0044
E-mail sales@arcadiapublishing.com
For customer service and orders:
Toll-Free 1-888-313-2665

Visit us on the Internet at www.arcadiapublishing.com

To my husband, Fulvio Manto, an aerospace and astronautics engineer who immigrated from Italy and began his career at Michoud Assembly Facility.

CONTENTS

ACKNOWLEDGMENTS

Special thanks to Irene Wainwright of the New Orleans Public Library, Cathy Miller of the National Archives, Robert Ticknor of The Historic New Orleans Collection, Kevin Kelly of The Boeing Company, Danielle Szostak of Chrysler Historical Services, Anne Coleman of the M. Louis Salmon Library at the University of Alabama in Huntsville, Matthew C. Hanson of the Franklin D. Roosevelt Presidential Library, Janice Davis of the Harry S. Truman Library, Kathy Struss of the Dwight D. Eisenhower Presidential Library and Museum, Sean Benjamin of the Louisiana Research Collection of the Howard-Tilton Memorial Library at Tulane University, Carl J. Howat of Jacobs Technology, and Sierra Nevada Corporation. Finally, thanks to Stephen A. Turner, emergency preparedness officer, and Malcolm W. Wood, deputy chief operating officer, both of NASA's Michoud Assembly Facility.

Many thanks to Mike Jetzer, the creator of heroicrelics.org; Jerry E. Strahan, *the* authority on all matters concerning Andrew Jackson Higgins; Robert B. Newton, a native of Great Britain, whose stories and engineering experience at Michoud began with Apollo and extended to the Space Shuttle era; and to Mary Ann Dutton, who moved to New Orleans for the External Tank and whose long friendship provided an insightful perspective into the shuttle era at Michoud. Thanks also to Kenneth J. Donze for his expertise in automobiles.

Please note that this is not an official publication of Jacobs Technology or NASA and that any opinions expressed or errors in content are the responsibility of the author.

—Cindy Donze Manto
Metairie, Louisiana

INTRODUCTION

Today's Michoud Assembly Facility was carved from a land grant to the wealthiest citizen in the Louisiana Territory on March 10, 1763. A successful businessman and commandant of the militia, Gilbert Antoine St. Maxent boldly requested 34,500 acres of land east of New Orleans from King Louis XV of France, along with exclusive trading rights with the local Native American tribes.

This land grant, or patent, was conditioned upon St. Maxent's ability to build a plantation on the property, bring a roadway across its width, and reserve all the trees for building or repairing royal ships. The French émigré continued to maintain his prominent position five years later, when the dominion came into Spanish possession, by merely changing his name to Gilberto Antonio St. Maxent.

Although the building or repairing of royal ships never occurred, an established plantation, including a road connecting St. Maxent's neighbor's property with his, "to a point called Chef Menteur," was in place at his death in 1796.

The Chef Menteur or "Chief Deceiver" was and still is a tidal estuary of Lake Borgne and the Gulf of Mexico whose misleading current flows either way with the tide. The Chef Menteur is the largest of several such estuaries in the area (the Rigolets, "small streams," is the other). It is a well-known landmark in the southeastern portion of this tract of land, offering entry into the interior of the large peninsula and a shorter route to the city of New Orleans.

During the final years of Spanish colonialism, this great expanse of land was acquired by the singular Lt. Louis Brognier DeClouet in 1796. A descendant of a prominent Creole family from St. Martinville, Louisiana, DeClouet was a militiaman and all around playboy in New Orleans. Harboring not-so-secret sympathies to Spain, Lieutenant DeClouet basically used his property to pay off gambling debts by selling off small parcels of it over time. Eventually, he sold the remainder of his land to another émigré from France and civil engineer for the City of New Orleans, Barthelemy Lafon.

An architect, theatrical promoter, cartographer, builder, appraiser, iron master and foundry owner, publisher, major in the militia, and "smuggler incognito" with the pirate Jean Lafitte, Lafon purchased the acreage in 1801. There, he continued the production of sugar at his plantation, now known as L'heureuse Folie ("Happy Folly"). After the Louisiana Territory was sold to the United States in 1804, Lafon immediately sought the legitimate recognition of his land ownership from the new government and proposed the use of the "chemin du Chef Menteur," the footpath that ran alongside the Chef Menteur, as a major mail route to Washington, DC, in 1805 for the sum of $3,500. This route would follow the Carondelet Canal out of the city to Gentilly Road, cross at Chef Menteur, and continue eastward into Mississippi and beyond. After demonstrating the convenience of establishing a direct route between New Orleans and Washington, DC, Lafon proposed the sale of the trees from his plantation to the US Navy for shipbuilding in 1812.

Between 1810 and 1815, Lafon surveyed the city's defenses and prepared fortifications on his property prior to the onset of the Battle of New Orleans. He chose the site and designed and built

7

Fort Petite Coquilles ("little shells") on the advice of his friend, Jean Lafitte, on the coast of Lake Pontchartrain to the north. However, Maj. Gen. Andrew Jackson complained that it was of little use protecting the Chef Menteur Pass between Lake Pontchartrain and Lake Catherine.

As the War of 1812 was about to end, continued reports of British troops circulating about the American Louisiana territory were becoming closer to reality when a British landing party was reportedly sighted at the Chef Menteur on Lafon's "Happy Folly" plantation on Christmas Day, 1814. Although the report proved to be false, General Jackson, for whom the British were constant enemies, ordered the "chemin du Chef Menteur" or Chef Menteur Road, fortified for military use should the British return upon the "Plains of Gentilly" and to serve as easy access into New Orleans. The British seizure of New Orleans could easily lead to an invasion of the United States proper from the south.

After the Battle of New Orleans was fought on January 8, 1815, at the village of Chalmette, less than 10 miles from the French Quarter, General Jackson ordered a redoubt at the confluence of Chef Menteur and Bayou Sauvage and completed and stationed a contingent of 450 free black troops there until he was certain that the British had left the coast.

Although what was now known as the "Lafon Tract" witnessed no battles to date, its strategic location as a defense of New Orleans was unquestioned. Fort Pike was completed in 1827 to guard over the Rigolets (a bayou that connects the eastern end of Lake Pontchartrain to Lake Borgne and the Mississippi Sound), and it still stands today.

Fort Macomb occupies a site on the western shore of the Chef Menteur Pass. Completed in 1822, it replaced an earlier post named Fort Chef Menteur. The rebuilt fort was renamed Fort Wood in 1822 and then Fort Macomb in 1851. (Fort Macomb sustained a large amount of damage from Hurricane Katrina in 2005). Both were part of Pres. James Monroe's extensive coastal defense system, protecting Lake Pontchartrain and, hence, the city of New Orleans from invasion forces from the east. Forts Jackson and St. Phillip defended the city near the mouth of the Mississippi River from the south.

Barthelemy Lafon died in 1820 during one of the almost yearly visits of yellow fever, and his large land holdings east of New Orleans passed first to his brother, then to his nieces and nephews, who sold it to yet another immigrant from France, Antoine Michoud, on October 3, 1827.

Michoud, whose father had served as administrator of domains in the province of Dauphine under Emperor Napoleon Bonaparte, was self-exiled to New Orleans after the emperor's fall in 1817. By then, New Orleans was becoming a prosperous American port city, and Michoud's fortune rose precipitously, including his appointment as the consul of the Kingdom of Sardinia and Savoy. Thereafter, he preferred to be addressed simply as "Chevalier."

Upon his arrival in New Orleans, Michoud opened an art and antiques shop on Royal Street and began buying several parcels of properties throughout the city, including the Lafon Tract, with its sugar plantation intact.

More important, he began to meticulously buy back the parcels of land that had been sold by the previous owners, once again amassing one of the largest privately held tracts of land in the nation. The plantation on the property continued to produce and refine sugar and a small amount of agricultural products for the local market.

Michoud also allowed the construction of the West Rigolets Lighthouse in 1855 to mark the entrance to the Rigolets from Lake Pontchartrain. During the Civil War, it was used by Union troops to signal passing ships. It remained in use until 1945. Eventually sold to a private owner, it was destroyed by Hurricane Katrina in 2005.

Although Michoud socialized with the leading aristocrats and entrepreneurs of the city, he grew increasingly reclusive. His French Quarter residence and business, now located at 520 Royal Street in the Seignouret House (the former home of WDSU-TV, the first television station in Louisiana in 1950), devolved into that of a junk dealer. Contemporary accounts characterize it as containing nothing but secondhand hardware and "barrels of rusty nails."

Antoine Michoud died alone in New Orleans on July 24, 1862, a little over one year after the start of the Civil War and following almost three months of Union occupation of the city. His plantation alone was appraised at $100,000 in the inventory of his estate. Michoud's properties passed first to his nephew Jean-Baptiste Michoud, a resident of Lyons, France. He died in 1877, leaving his inheritance to his son Marie-Alphonse Michoud. Both retained lawyers in New Orleans to oversee their numerous properties, especially the Michoud Plantation. Both never traveled to New Orleans or anywhere in the United States during their lifetimes.

However, both father and son sold rights-of-way over the years as the demand for transportation and communication increased. A 100-foot right-of-way for a railroad that would later become the Louisville & Nashville Railroad Company was sold in 1870, while a site for the Point-aux-Herbes Lighthouse was sold to the US government in 1877. Another right-of-way was sold to the predecessor of the Southern Railway System in 1882. In 1900, the American Telephone and Telegraph Company bought a right-of-way for land lines.

The Michoud Tract remained virtually intact despite these small sales, and in 1910, Marie-Alphonse Michoud sold the entire, immense tract east of New Orleans to John Stuart Watson for $410,000 in cash. Watson then sold it to his firm, the New Orleans Drainage Company, on the same day for the same amount in cash.

Not surprisingly, this began a period of defaults, sales, and questionable ownership titles, ending with ownership by the Continental & Commercial Trust & Savings Bank in Chicago. The enormous property was bought on June 12, 1923, for $1 million with terms and a down payment that had been borrowed by Col. Roch Eugene Edgar de Montluzin du Sauzay, a descendant of French aristocrats. The entire tract was now formally named Faubourg deMontluzin ("Suburb deMontluzin"), and the remains of the plantation on the property are known only as Michoud Plantation.

Better known as Col. R.E.E. deMontluzin, the colonel had already developed a large parcel of land, in an area known as Gentilly (after the Paris suburb), into Gentilly Terrace. The residential development comprised variously shaped and sized California bungalow, English Tudor, and Spanish hacienda homes whose distinguishing feature was their construction on raised terraces above street level. Today, Gentilly Terrace is a historic district listed in the National Register of Historic Places.

With the purchase of the Michoud Tract, Colonel deMontluzin now owned approximately one-fourth of the land area of the corporate city of New Orleans, most of it swamps. However, he steadfastly saw the possibilities of residential and commercial development farther east of New Orleans proper. During the Depression years, he withheld the type of development of his previous endeavors and instead sold trees for railroad cross ties, leased the marshlands to muskrat trappers, and sold rights-of-way for power and telephone lines and for outdoor advertising billboards along the new Chef Menteur Highway, paved in 1927 to become part of US Highway 90. The colonel then granted permission to the US government to build the Intracoastal Canal through the southern portion of his property as an alternative route to the Gulf of Mexico.

On the eve of World War II, Colonel deMontluzin sold nearly 1,000 acres along the southern part of Faubourg deMontluzin for $174,221.66 in cash to the US government. Under the auspices of the US Maritime Commission, Higgins Industries of New Orleans was awarded a contract to build a facility for the fabrication of Liberty ships in the vicinity of the former Michoud Plantation, a mere 15 miles from the New Orleans French Quarter, for the impending war effort.

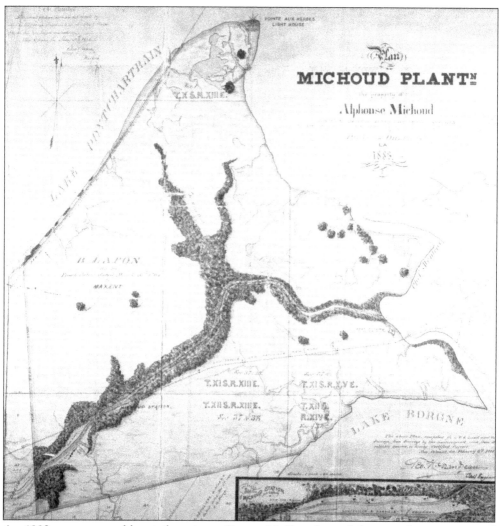

An 1883 map prepared by civil engineer George N. Grandjean delineates the property and improvements made to the plantation of Antoine Michoud's great-grandnephew and current owner, Marie-Alphonse Michoud. It was later used for identification for the 1910 act of sale to John Stuart Watson, who sold it to his New Orleans Drainage Company on the same day. (Courtesy of NASA.)

One

WORLD WAR II
AND HIGGINS
1940–1950

The Higgins Shipyard at Michoud was originally conceived as one of several strategic countrywide locations for the fabrication of Liberty ships. Construction began in 1941 but was abruptly shut down by the US Maritime Commission shortly afterward on the pretense of a nationwide shortage of steel. However, Pres. Franklin D. Roosevelt was adamant that some defense use be found for the partially completed industrial plant.

By October 1942, Higgins Industries was awarded a contract to build 1,200 C-76 Curtiss Caravans made of molded plywood. These planes would be the wood-alloy version of the metal C-46 Commando cargo planes built for the US Army Air Force. Additionally, Higgins Industries would fabricate wing panels for the Curtiss-Wright C-46 plants in Louisville, Kentucky, and St. Louis, Missouri.

Construction began anew on the Michoud Industrial Plant, including assurances by Andrew Jackson Higgins to a local historic preservationist that the old sugar refinery smokestacks would be stabilized and preserved as part of a small park.

The Michoud Aircraft Plant was dedicated on October 24, 1943. Manufacturing had already begun several weeks before, utilizing Higgins's unconventional yet innovative assembly line methods designed to support economies of scale and commonality. Higgins offered training and employment to persons regardless of gender or color and to the able and the partially disabled. Transportation was provided to anyone who lived within 100 miles of a Higgins plant.

As emphasis shifted from cargo to long-range troop transport for the war effort, the C-46 contract was cancelled after only two planes were produced. But Higgins Aircraft continued to produce subassemblies of wing panels. The plant's unused aircraft hangar was then used to restore thousands of US Army jeeps and trucks. Also, Higgins Plastics continued to produce airborne lifeboats, while Higgins Carbon Division supposedly produced radar and radio communication equipment. In reality, the "Carbonites" were machining millions of graphite and stainless-steel parts for the electromagnetic separation of uranium 235 for the first atomic bomb.

World War II ended on September 2, 1945. By 1946, the War Assets Administration deemed Michoud to be registered surplus.

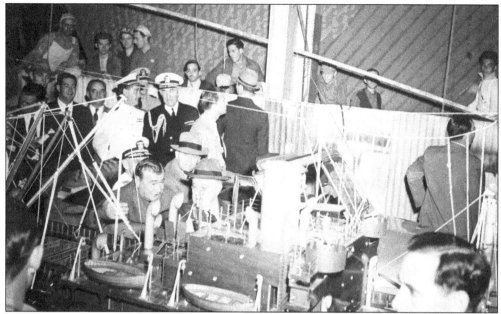

Andrew Jackson Higgins (lower left) explains the capabilities of his shipyards to Pres. Franklin D. Roosevelt in front of a Liberty ship model during the president's only visit to the City Park facility of Higgins Industries. Seated behind Higgins and the president are Rear Adm. Frank T. Leighton (left) and Louisiana governor Sam Houston Jones. (Courtesy of Franklin D. Roosevelt Presidential Library.)

Materials are rapidly deployed as construction continues on the Michoud Aircraft Plant on May 15, 1943. The Defense Plant Corporation leased Michoud to Higgins Aircraft for $1 per year. (Courtesy of NASA.)

Date 8-15-4

Completed ahead of schedule and under budget, Buildings 101 (upper right), 102 (center), and 103 (left) await opening-day ceremonies in August 1943. Building 103 alone contained 1.86 million square feet, with a floor-to-ceiling truss height of 40 feet. (Courtesy of NASA.)

The "flying box cars," the only two C-76 Curtiss Caravans built at Michoud, near completion on August 15, 1944. (Courtesy of NASA.)

Shown here is one of two Curtiss-Wright C-46 Commando cargo planes built for the US Army Air Force. It awaits final assembly in Building 103 under strict security. (Courtesy of Jerry E. Strahan.)

Higgins Industries also provided wing subassemblies, shown here in cross-section, to Curtiss-Wright C-46 plants in Louisville and St. Louis. (Courtesy of Jerry E. Strahan.)

Dec. 31, 1944

Higgins Plastics mass-produced approximately 600 airborne lifeboats, some of which are seen here on December 31, 1944. Production was achieved using a giant autoclave on-site. The air-sea boat was carried under the belly of the Boeing B-17 Bomber and released by parachute at 1,500 feet. (Courtesy of NASA.)

Two

THE KOREAN WAR AND CHRYSLER CORPORATION
1950–1960

Notwithstanding the uncertainty during the years following World War II, the Michoud Industrial Plant proved to be adaptable to new uses. After its declaration as surplus in 1946, the New Orleans Port Commission purchased Michoud on November 28, 1947. Andrew Jackson Higgins purchased the plywood and veneer plant nearby and leased 400,000 square feet of the plant itself for new business ventures. The port commission leased the now-subdivided facility to several local businesses.

Inundation and significant damage to the property was caused by an unnamed hurricane earlier that year. The port commission endorsed plans to levee the 20 square miles of land surrounding the plant. This critical improvement proved to be timely, as Pres. Harry S. Truman called for an "urgent and intense" defense-production drive to counter Communist aggression in Korea in 1951. The Army Ordnance Procurement Agency promptly served a 30-day notice to vacate on Michoud tenants.

Chrysler Corporation, through the ordnance division of its engineering department, had been awarded a $100 million tank-engine contract and had already built a new tank plant in Newark, Delaware. At Michoud, the corporation instituted an employee-training program and retooled the facility at a cost of several million dollars. The plant now produced tank cylinder heads, later manufacturing 12-cylinder engines for Sherman tanks and the new Patton 48 medium tanks.

Defense conversion also included a block-long test cell structure and a tank farm for storage of gasoline and oil used in building and testing engines. Aerial photographs revealed thousands of pilings beneath the plant floor, in contrast to the two old smokestacks.

The Michoud plant shipped the first carload of New Orleans–built tank engines in a record 11 months. The engines were destined for installation at the Chrylser Delaware Tank Plant.

Production ended in March 1954. The US Army spent approximately $550,000 annually to keep the plant on standby but by 1958 deemed the expenditure to be a waste of money. In 1960, the US government made a large parcel available to the New Orleans Sewerage & Water Board for a sewerage disposal facility in anticipation of the increasing residential development of the surrounding area.

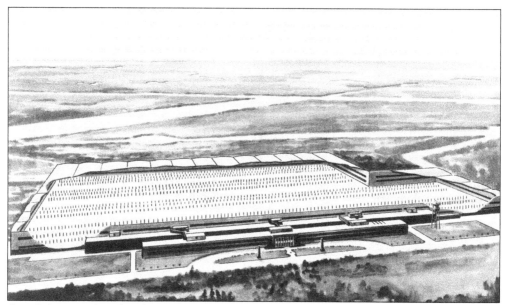

Aerial photographs taken during construction revealed the presence of more than 20,000 pilings beneath the building. Chrysler altered plant layouts to utilize these pilings in building foundations for the heavier machines and equipment, saving taxpayers $1 million and accelerating the conversion to defense production. (Courtesy of Chrysler Historical Collection.)

The Michoud Ordnance Plant was prepared to produce a 12-cylinder, air-cooled, V-type engine weighing 2,600 pounds and developing 810 horsepower. The engine was designed to power the Army's new medium Patton M47 and Patton M48 tanks and its giant T-43 heavy tank. (Courtesy of Chrysler Historical Collection.)

Chrysler officials stand beside a partially completed engine assembly in 1953. Visible beneath the engine buggy is the underground track, the latest in conveyor equipment that tows the buggies along the assembly line at speeds of from nine inches to two feet per minute. (Courtesy of NASA.)

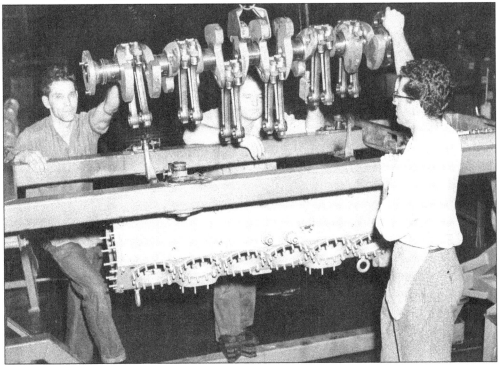

Technicians take time out as they stand with a partially assembled crankshaft with pistons and flywheel mounted on an engine buggy as it moves along the assembly line. (Courtesy of NASA.)

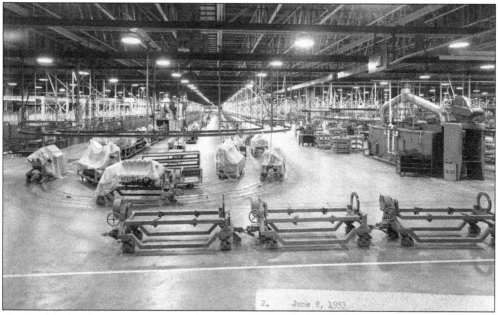

During the plant's reconversion, a steel grillage was installed over the entire manufacturing area, bringing the truss height to 18 feet. Some 27,000 feet of overhead conveyors were installed, 4,800 feet of floor conveyors, and 500 miles of electrical wiring. This June 8, 1953, photograph shows the final assembly area. The "green line," one of two main assembly lines, is on the right, and the "tear down/build-up" line is on the left. (Courtesy of NASA.)

Officials from Chrysler Corporation and US Army Ordnance gather in 1953 to show off their newly manufactured 12-cylinder, air-cooled engine, "more powerful than six average car engines." (Courtesy of NASA.)

20

As military and civilian onlookers stand by in front of the Pontalba Apartments facing Jackson Square, in the heart of the New Orleans French Quarter, technicians lower a completed engine onto a truck. This publicity photograph was designed to clearly indicate where Chrysler Corporation was manufacturing its tank engines. (Courtesy of NASA.)

Shown here on August 31, 1954, is a portion of the 2,400 machines on standby status after production ended in March of that year. Improvements to the plant included a 9,900-ton dehumidification system designed to maintain temperature at 80 degrees and relative humidity at 50 percent. Other features included an aluminum foundry capable of pouring over three million pounds of aluminum per month and a by-products reclamation system. (Author's collection.)

MICHOUD ASSEMBLY FACILITY
HISTORY OF UTILIZATION

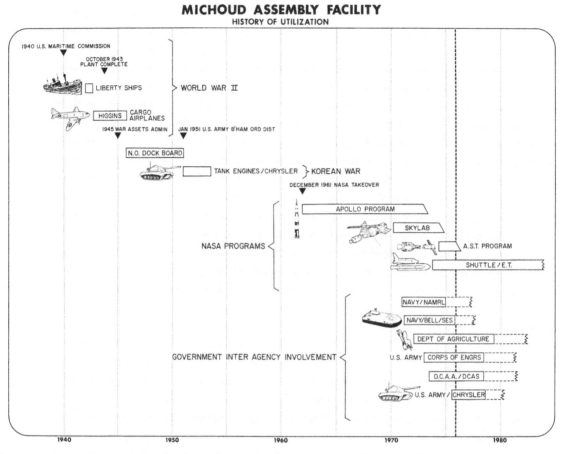

This chart illustrates 40 years of government interagency involvement at Michoud, beginning with the US Maritime Commission and ending with NASA by 1980. (Courtesy of NASA.)

Three

APOLLO ARRIVES
1961–1972

As the Cold War heated up following World War II, the US Department of Defense developed an increasing interest in rocketry and its varied uses. As a result, on July 29, 1958, Pres. Dwight D. Eisenhower signed the National Aeronautics and Space Act, dissolving the National Advisory Committee for Aeronautics (NACA), which had been founded in 1915, and creating the National Aeronautics and Space Administration (NASA).

Almost immediately, new field installations were established, especially the George C. Marshall Space Flight Center on the grounds of the US Army's Redstone Arsenal in Huntsville, Alabama. Dr. Wernher von Braun, an early advocate of liquid-fuel boosters and an eight-engine, clustered tank configuration, became its first director. Dr. von Braun viewed the accelerating space race in terms of a national emergency and urged Pres. John F. Kennedy to consider that "we are competing with a determined opponent whose peacetime economy is on a wartime footing." After the Soviet Union achieved the first manned flight into space, Kennedy issued a virtual mandate to put a man on the moon by the end of the decade. Congress supported the new space program with a large budget increase for the Apollo Manned Lunar Flight Project, and facility planning was given high-priority status.

NASA asked the General Services Administration to suspend its disposal of Michoud for 120 days, allowing von Braun to inspect the facility on June 6, 1961. The site was readily available, with access to navigable waterways and with 43 acres under one climate-controlled roof, and it required little modification. NASA was heavily lobbied by New Orleans mayor Victor H. Schiro and a local citizens committee to activate the facility. In September, NASA announced the takeover of Michoud.

Known as Michoud Operations, the site became part of a "space crescent" that included the Mississippi Test Operations (later renamed the John C. Stennis Space Center) near the town of Kiln in Hancock County, and Cape Canaveral in Florida, all under administrative control of the George C. Marshall Space Flight Center in Huntsville, Alabama.

Dr. Wernher von Braun (left) provides an animated description of the Saturn Space Vehicle, shown here in one-tenth scale, to Pres. Dwight D. Eisenhower. The occasion was the dedication of the George C. Marshall Space Flight Center in Huntsville, Alabama, on September 8, 1960. (Courtesy of the Dwight D. Eisenhower Presidential Library.)

NASA's search for additional field installations touched off intense lobbying among the nation's cities. New Orleans mayor Victor H. Schiro (front row, center) formed an all-male, but racially inclusive, NASA–New Orleans Coordinating Committee to showcase the ability of the Michoud Industrial Plant to meet the space agency's needs. Some members of the committee gathered in Huntsville, Alabama, to await the results of NASA's final decision. (Courtesy of the New Orleans Public Library.)

After the announcement of the new George C. Marshall Space Flight Center Michoud Operations, NASA held an all-day subcontractor bidders' conference in New Orleans, ending in a gala banquet sponsored by the New Orleans Chamber of Commerce in the Grand Ballroom of the Roosevelt Hotel in the Central Business District. Dr. Wernher von Braun (at the podium) addresses the audience on December 11, 1961. (Courtesy of the New Orleans Public Library.)

In appreciation for allowing the city of New Orleans to help the nation "get to the moon a day sooner," Mayor Victor H. Schiro (right) presented Dr. Wernher von Braun with a proclamation declaring December 11 "Wernher von Braun Day" in New Orleans. (Courtesy of the New Orleans Public Library.)

Dr. von Braun (right) presents Mayor Schiro with a model of Saturn I. Afterward, von Braun wrote, "Frankly, I don't believe that I have ever been associated with a more friendly, effective and helpful group of people than you and your fellow citizens in New Orleans and Louisiana. And, I should like to thank you for the many fine courtesies extended to me and my colleagues of the Marshall Center." (Courtesy of the New Orleans Public Library.)

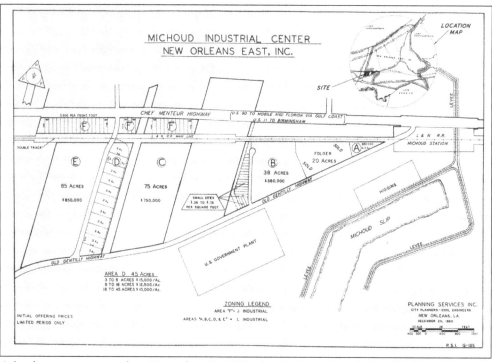

A land-use map prepared on December 29, 1960, clearly shows the Michoud Industrial Center, complete with its own docks, levee, and highway access. Michoud was at the center of the anticipated development of the commercial and residential area surrounding it just east of downtown New Orleans. (Courtesy of the New Orleans Public Library.)

Advertisers and businesses, large and small, sought to take advantage of the economic stroke of luck that had just ushered New Orleans into the space race. An outdoor billboard company tore the headlines from the local newspaper for use in a mailer to its customers in 1961. (Courtesy of the New Orleans Public Library.)

This aerial photograph, taken on the eve of NASA's takeover of the facility, shows the iconic smokestacks set before Buildings 101, 102, and 103 (center). The airfield is at upper right, and the Intracoastal Canal is visible across the background. By 1966, a separate engineering and administrative building, a vertical assembly structure, enlarged barge facilities, and other miscellaneous support buildings had been added to the site. (Courtesy of the New Orleans Public Library.)

A sign sporting a stylized Saturn Space Vehicle points the way to the entrance of the newly built Michoud Boulevard, "serving the Saturn Booster Plant." The road led all visitors to the main gate after passing a great deal of much-hoped-for industrial concerns along the way. (Courtesy of the New Orleans Public Library.)

The newly appointed manager of NASA-Michoud Operation, Dr. George C. Constan, stands before the main entrance to Building 101, an administrative office that faces Old Gentilly Road. Dr. Constan was an original member of Dr. Wernher von Braun's Initial Management Structure for the George C. Marshall Space Flight Center in 1960. Constan served as head of the technical program in the coordination office. (Courtesy of the New Orleans Public Library.)

Mayor Schiro (seated, center) and Congressman Thomas Hale Boggs (standing, second from left) meet with a group of Boeing Company executives and labor representatives. Boggs, a Democrat, represented the Second Congressional District of Louisiana, where Michoud is located. (Courtesy of the Victor Schiro Papers, Louisiana Research Collection, Tulane University.)

The NASA-New Orleans Coordinating Committee's public relations machine went into action, as tours and informational brochures were disseminated throughout the city. A group of dignitaries visited the future booster factory while its reactivation was under way on August 8, 1962. (Courtesy of NASA.)

Dr. Wernher von Braun was an eloquent and persuasive spokesperson for America's emerging space program. On September 11, 1962, eighteen months after President Kennedy's speech regarding a manned mission to the moon, von Braun (left) gave Kennedy a personal tour of the facilities at George C. Marshall Space Flight Center in Huntsville, Alabama. The flight center had mock-ups of Saturn IB and various rocket engines. (Author's collection.)

Dr. George Constan, manager of Michoud Operations (center), and Congressman F. Edward Hebert, Democrat, First Congressional District (left), tour the grounds with an unidentified visitor as additional building projects are under way. (Courtesy of NASA.)

An exhibition of the newly acquired economic plum was on display on South Rampart Street in the Central Business District in New Orleans. Shown here are, from left to right, James J. Coleman, chairman, NASA-New Orleans Coordinating Committee; Congressman F. Edward Hebert; and Mayor Victor H. Schiro. (Courtesy of NASA.)

Stepping out from a 1962 Chrysler Imperial LeBaron during a visit to Michoud in February 1962 are Dr. George Constan, manager of Michoud Operations (left), and Dr. Wernher von Braun, director of NASA's George C. Marshall Space Flight Center in Huntsville, Alabama. An unidentified security guard is at right. Behind them is one of the sugar refinery smokestacks and Old Gentilly Road. (Courtesy of NASA.)

Surrounded by officials from Chrysler Corporation and The Boeing Company, Dr. von Braun (third from left) enters the main portal to Building 101, an administrative building. (Courtesy of NASA.)

Dr. George Constan (left) and Dr. Wernher von Braun survey the newly refurbished interior of Building 101. (Courtesy of NASA.)

Dr. Constan (foreground) and Dr. von Braun (rear, right) proceed to walk the full length of Building 101, accompanied by executives from Chrysler Corporation and The Boeing Company and members of the media. (Courtesy of NASA.)

Dr. von Braun (second from left) and others listen intently to a representative from Mason-Rust, the facilities management company contracted by NASA to operate the Michoud facility. The speaker is detailing the full use of the entire 844.22 acres, including office space, manufacturing space, general spaces, and parking lots. (Courtesy of NASA.)

Wernher von Braun (second from left) and other NASA officials view schematic drawings of the overall layout of the facility. Note the glass ashtray used as a weight on the table. (Courtesy of NASA.)

Shown here at a meet and greet at Michoud are, from left to right, an unidentified visitor; Congressman F. Edward Hebert; Dr. Wernher von Braun, director of George C. Marshall Space Flight Center; Mayor Victor H. Schiro; and James J. Coleman, chairman, NASA-New Orleans Coordinating Committee. (Courtesy of the New Orleans Public Library.)

Mayor Victor H. Schiro's official 1962 Christmas card depicted Santa Claus with a bag full of rockets slung over his shoulder. His feet are planted firmly in downtown New Orleans, with the Mississippi River flowing behind him. Santa points confidently to the great promise of science and rocketry taking shape just 15 miles to the east of downtown New Orleans. (Courtesy of the New Orleans Public Library.)

Mabel Brouwer, an employee of the New Orleans Lighthouse for the Blind, reads in Braille *A Trip to the Moon in Project Apollo* in 1966. The brochure was prepared by the Public Affairs Office of NASA's Michoud Assembly Facility and distributed to hundreds of blind persons in the United States and around the world. (Courtesy of the National Archives.)

Mayor Victor H. Schiro (center) and executives from Airco Company preside over ground-breaking ceremonies for the construction of the new Airco plant at Michoud on March 18, 1964. (Courtesy of the Victor Schiro Papers, Louisiana Collection, Tulane University.)

Completed in 1964, this is the first of several buildings to house subcontractors for Saturn booster rockets at Michoud. Space Harness, Inc., supplied cable harnesses used to connect various electrical systems specific to the needs of space exploration. (Courtesy of the New Orleans Public Library.)

With smiles all around, and each man sporting his own boutonniere, four New Orleans city councilmen take part in the ribbon-cutting ceremony for Space Harness, Inc. Shown here are, from left to right, Chad Farris, Urban Wilkinson, Dan Kelly, and Lloyd F. Gaubert. (Courtesy of the New Orleans Public Library.)

This is a rendering of Building 350 by August Perez and Associates of New Orleans. Commonly referred to as the "H" Building, it was part of the expanding facilities construction that provided space for engineering and administrative activities. (Courtesy of NASA.)

This is an overhead view of the nearly completed and much-anticipated Vehicle Assembly Building (VAB). The VAB is, technically, a single-story structure that rises to the equivalent of 18 stories. A 180-ton overhead crane stacks the five large cylindrical segments of the first stage booster into a vertical assembly position. (Courtesy of NASA.)

The final assembly of the propellant tanks and the joining of the major components into the complete stage will occur in the VAB, shown here under construction. (Courtesy of NASA.)

A well-suited visitor surveys a suited-up astronaut and a display detailing the intricacies of manned space flight in the lobby of the newly completed Building 350, or "H" Building. (Courtesy of the New Orleans Public Library.)

The Saturn Proposal Group for The Boeing Company gathers around a display of a Saturn V first-stage rocket booster, or S-IB. The group's "S-IB Master Phasing Schedule," seen on the blackboard, included nine decision parameters, including the following: stage design, Michoud Plant activation, stage manufacturing, stage quality control and systems checkout, ground support, and launch operations. (Courtesy of The Boeing Company.)

Before production began, The Boeing Company, a prime contractor, constructed a full-scale model of the Saturn V booster (S-IC). The size, angle, and other measurements of tubes and wires were to be determined from the model, and this information was used in production of flight vehicles. Nearly reaching the top of the 40-foot bay, the SI-C weighed 4,687,000 pounds when fully fueled with liquid oxygen and kerosene. (Courtesy of the National Archives.)

A scale model of the Saturn V rocket booster dwarfs a technician in Building 103. This engineering prototype is shown with one of the five F-1 engines in position on the aft end of the vehicle. (Author's collection.)

Here, two executives from The Boeing Company view a full-scale mock-up of the fuel-tank bulkhead of the Saturn V first-stage rocket booster. Robert J. Murphy, vice president and manager of the firm's Washington, DC, office, is at left. With him is R.H. Nelson, general manager at Boeing's Michoud Plant. A total of four bulkheads were used in the boosters. (Author's collection.)

This dome structure, with all the gore segments welded together and the resulting bulkhead welded to the Y-ring, undergoes a chemical process administered by two Boeing Company technicians. This process is one of several types of sprays, washes, and rinses the individual components were subjected to before becoming part of the complete Saturn V booster rocket. (Courtesy of The Boeing Company.)

The final cleaning area of one of three clean-room complexes contains plastic packaged components ready for use in the Saturn V first stage. The clean rooms were designed to prevent contamination of the propellant system components. (Author's collection.)

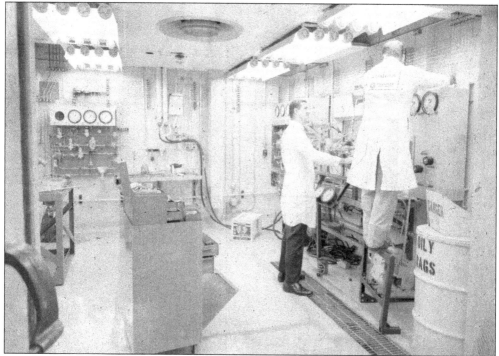

Technicians with prime contractor Chrysler Corporation work inside the Static Test Tower in September 1965, when the S-IB-2 through S-IB-5 were at Michoud. (Courtesy of NASA.)

Chrysler technicians attend to their duties as dictated by the two large magnetic-tape drive cabinets (left). The cabinets to the right of the computers are strip recorders, similar to seismograph machines. (Courtesy of NASA.)

Technicians are at work on a quarter dome mounted on a weld track, used for dome-weld tooling. This photograph was taken on October 24, 1963. (Courtesy of NASA.)

Boeing Company technicians cover the edges of a fuel-tank section with aluminum to protect the surface from contamination until another section is welded in place. The 33-foot-diameter dome will cap a fuel tank in the first stage of the Saturn V rocket. (Author's collection.)

Technicians inspect a Saturn I or IB thrust structure. Michoud manufactured two S-I stages, plus the first two S-IB stages. Both were manufactured largely to S-I specifications. The thrust structure is part of the tail unit assembly at the aft end of the S-I or S-IB stage. (Courtesy of the New Orleans Public Library.)

A group of employees from Chrysler Corporation ride a tour tram to survey the fabrication of 70-inch fuel tanks and 70-inch liquid oxygen (LOX) tanks. Chrysler was particularly proud of the innovative clustering formation of these fuel tanks for its Saturn S-I booster. (Courtesy of Mike Jetzer of heroicrelics.org.)

A technician stands next to a 70-inch LOX tank built by Chrysler Corporation. The precision requirements of the S-I manufacture dictate assembly within tolerances of a few thousandths of an inch. (Courtesy of the New Orleans Public Library.)

The major steps in the clustering operation are positioning the tail unit, attaching the 105-inch LOX tank and spider beam, and positioning the eight remaining LOX and fuel tanks. (Courtesy of NASA.)

The top photograph shows the amount of immense, unobstructed space the Michoud facility offered. To fabricate and assemble the lower stages of a Saturn rocket required a huge manufacturing plant. The bottom photograph illustrates how the manufacture of the Saturn boosters completely filled that space. Awaiting final assembly are a pair of S-I boosters, with their spider beams visible. Once clustering operations are completed, the remaining operations include the installation of tubing, measurement instruments, and the rocket engines. The booster will be given a complete functional checkout, prepared for shipment, and shipped to Huntsville for static firing. It has been said that no other facility could accommodate such large launch-vehicle stages. (Courtesy of NASA.)

This 1966 photograph of the production facilities of the Chrysler Corporation shows first stages of the uprated Saturn launch vehicle in various phases of assembly. The technicians are inspecting an H-1 rocket engine (lower right), the type used in the S-I and S-IB stages. This version is an inboard H-1 engine and sports a partial aspirator, or exhaust duct. (Courtesy of Harry S. Truman Presidential Library.)

In this 1966 photograph, Chrysler Corporation technicians put the finishing touches on the first Saturn IB booster. The stage is 80 feet long, 21.5 feet in diameter, and weighs some 85,000 pounds. The primary mission of the S-IB booster was to launch the Apollo spacecraft and S-I VB stage into low-Earth orbit for spacecraft testing and astronaut training. (Courtesy of the National Archives.)

This postcard shows five Saturn I and Saturn IB first stages lined up in final assembly and checkout positions. The Saturn I boosters, providing 1.5 million pounds of thrust, were used in the early phases of the Apollo manned lunar landing program. The more-powerful 1.6-million-pound-thrust Saturn IB first stages launched Apollo spacecraft into orbit for astronaut training and spacecraft tests prior to manned moon landings. (Author's collection.)

H-1 Engines Awaiting Installation at MAF - 1967

A baker's dozen of H-1 rocket engines built by North American Aviation's Rocketdyne Division near Canoga Park, California, wait in storage for installation in August 1967. (Courtesy of Mike Jetzer of heroicrelics.org.)

Shown here is the arrival by barge of an F-1 rocket engine from the Santa Susana Field Laboratory of North American Aviation's Rocketdyne Division near Canoga Park, California, in 1968. (Courtesy of NASA.)

These visitors touring the Michoud facility on July 19, 1967, wear jackets, ties, and hard hats but not necessarily identification badges. The men are taking in the immense production area of Building 103. (Courtesy of the New Orleans Public Library.)

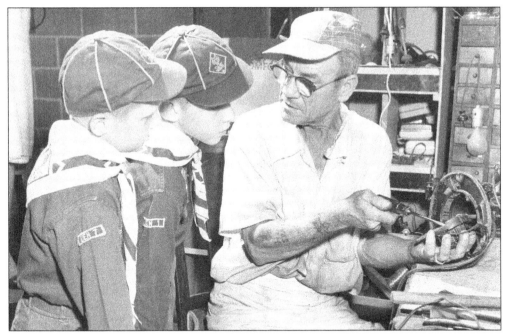

A technician patiently explains bench mechanics to two New Orleans–area Boy Scouts visiting Michoud. The public was encouraged to arrange guided tours for their clubs, organizations, or schools as a way to learn about, and maintain public support for, the space program. (Courtesy of the New Orleans Public Library.)

Executives watch as technicians install one of five F-1 engines in a Saturn first stage, or SI-C booster, in a cluster formation. Here, four of the engines are mounted on a 364-inch-diameter ring and gimbaled for control purposes. The fifth engine is rigidly mounted in the center. The bicycle at lower right is the transportation of choice at Michoud. (Courtesy of NASA.)

Under watchful eyes, an F-1 rocket engine is moved into place by crane in December 1967. Optical alignment was often just as important as precision alignment. (Courtesy of NASA.)

A Boeing Company technician installs an F-1 rocket engine built by North American Aviation's Rocketdyne Division. The single-chamber F-1 used liquid oxygen (LOX) and RP-1, a kerosene. It was the largest and most powerful liquid fuel rocket engine ever built. (Courtesy of NASA.)

A technician inspecting an F-1 rocket engine as it rests on its transporter is dwarfed by its massive size. F-1 rocket engines were static-fired many times at full thrust for the full duration of two and a half minutes before shipment to Michoud. (Courtesy of the New Orleans Public Library.)

Technicians process a shipment of three H-1 engines. The near engine is an inboard engine, which lacks the aspirator. The dark, teardrop-shaped component just above the right shoulder of the technician at center is the liquid propellant gas generator, used to power the turboprop. (Author's collection.)

A second-stage SI-C booster receives interim inspections before its five J-2 engines are installed. (Courtesy of NASA.)

A Saturn V launch vehicle undergoes final assembly in Building 103. "Saturn" is the generic name for large launch vehicles related to the Apollo program. "Apollo" was used by NASA to describe all large space-launch vehicles. It has been deemed "the most famous name in space exploration." (Courtesy of NASA.)

A Boeing technician wrangles a thrust structure in the Vehicle Assembly Building. Located at the base of the stage, the thrust structure provides support for the engines, engine accessories, and the fin and fairing assemblies. (Courtesy of the New Orleans Public Library.)

Boeing technicians work inside the SI-C LOX tank. This photograph was taken from the forward end of the tank, looking aft at its cruciform anti-vortex baffle. The anti-slosh baffles are the components that are thigh-high to the technicians, mounted on the tank wall. The helium tanks are also mounted to the tank wall, run through the baffles, and are routed through the F-1 engines' heat exchangers. (Courtesy of The Boeing Company.)

The last of the Saturn IB boosters takes shape in the spring of 1969. NASA originally ordered 12 of the first stages, finally increasing the order by two. A booster of this type helped launch the first three-man Apollo crew into Earth's orbit on October 11, 1968. (Courtesy of the National Archives.)

The first stage of the Apollo/Saturn launch vehicle undergoes final checks in 1966 before leaving Michoud in New Orleans. It had been static-tested at NASA's George C. Marshall Space Flight Center in Huntsville, Alabama. The 80-foot-long SI-B stage has eight H-1 engines built by North American Aviation's Rocketdyne Division and produces a total thrust of 1.6 million pounds. (Courtesy of the National Archives.)

A completed S-IC booster, the first stage of the Saturn V moon rocket manufactured by The Boeing Company, is lifted from its final assembly position in the 215-foot-high Vertical Assembly Building (VAB). Technicians are in the process of lowering the 138-foot stage to the floor and onto a custom-made transporter. (Author's collection.)

This photograph sequence, taken over six weeks, shows the major steps, from left to right, in assembling the first stage of the Saturn V. The first photograph shows the thrust structure, which supports the rocket's weight and distributes engine forces. In the second image is the 203,000-gallon fuel tank. Next, the intertank acts as a spacer between the fuel and liquid oxygen tank. In the fourth photograph, the LOX tank is joined to the engines by five "tunnels." Finally, the forward skirt tops the first stage. (Courtesy of the New Orleans Public Library.)

Boeing technicians prepare a Saturn V first-stage booster for a move from its vertical assembly position. Each S-IC stage spent only two and a half minutes in flight. (Courtesy of The Boeing Company.)

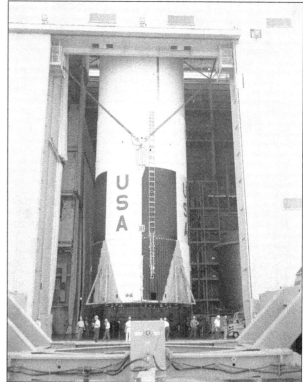

This photograph shows the VAB, Cell A, on June 7, 1971. A Saturn SI-C booster has been stacked and bolted and is about to be laid horizontally onto its transporter (foreground). (Courtesy of NASA.)

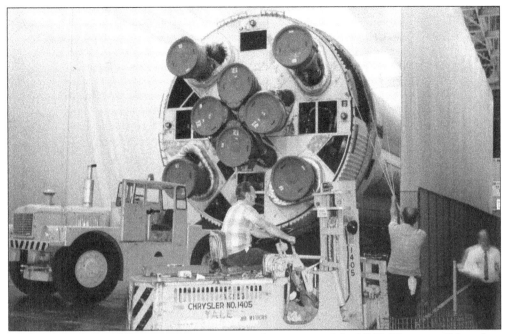

A "Move Crew" carefully prepares to transport a booster out of the VAB. Then, it will be taken to the Michoud slip for water transport. (Courtesy of NASA.)

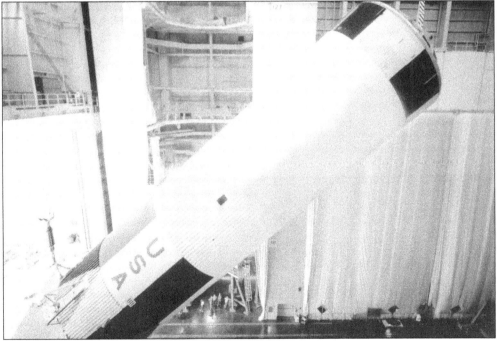

A Saturn V booster is being prepared to leave the VAB and return to the production area of Building 103. The base of the stage (left) is attached to a fixed-hinge system, which is stretched across the door. A crane then lowers the upper end (right) into the horizontal position and onto the transporter. The first-stage booster had its own specially built transporter, 195 feet long and 38 feet wide. (Author's collection.)

An intertank, the second component of the booster stack, is shown here en route to the VAB for final assembly. (Courtesy of NASA.)

The "Move Crew" was composed of a group of highly skilled employees responsible for getting the boosters where they needed to go without damage to the booster itself. The boosters traveled from the manufacturing sites to the VAB, then to the SI-C Stage Test Facility, and eventually to the barge dock for delivery to Cape Canaveral and, ultimately, liftoff. (Courtesy of NASA.)

Technicians work on electronic components in the subassembly area of Building 103. In the distance at center, the boosters are visible. (Courtesy of the New Orleans Public Library.)

On July 6, 1965, George C. Marshall Space Flight Center Michoud Operations was officially renamed Michoud Assembly Facility to "better reflect the mission" of the facility. The VAB is to the right of the sign. (Courtesy of the New Orleans Public Library.)

Guided tours were facilitated by a 24-passenger tour train, seen here passing two Saturn IB boosters. In 1965, Michoud was one of Louisiana's major attractions, with more than 30,000 visitors. (Author's collection.)

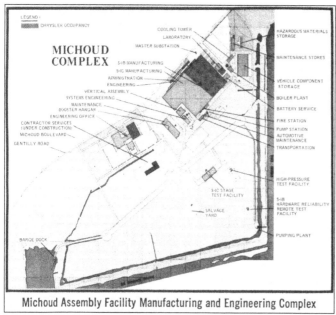

Michoud Assembly Facility Manufacturing and Engineering Complex

By the mid-1960s, improvements to Michoud that had been on the drawing board only a few years earlier were built and in full use at the height of the space race. (Courtesy of Mike Jetzer of heroicrelics.org.)

Dr. Wernher von Braun (left) and NASA administrator James Webb (right) look on approvingly as Pres. Lyndon B. Johnson strikes a high note during a speech at Michoud on December 13, 1967. (Author's collection.)

President Johnson addresses employees and dignitaries during his tour of Michoud. Seated behind Johnson are Gov. John J. McKeithen of Louisiana (left of center), Patsy Webb (center), and NASA administrator James Webb (right). (Courtesy of Harry S. Truman Presidential Library.)

Annual open houses at Michoud served to showcase "the security which comes from U.S. leadership in space." Here, an array of Saturn engines is on display for the public. At left is an H-1 engine, designed for use in boosters in clusters of eight. At center is an F-1 engine, which powers the first stage of Saturn V. At right is a J-2 engine, which steered both second and third stages of Saturn V. (Courtesy of NASA.)

Competition among the field installations operated by George C. Marshall Space Flight Center involved merit and idea awards as well as sports and beauty pageants. The 1966–1967 pageant sponsored by the Marshall Athletic, Recreational, and Social (MARS) Association was won by Susan Bauduc, an employee of NASA at the Michoud Assembly Facility in New Orleans. She received a US Savings Bond, a large trophy, and a bouquet of roses from Dr. Wernher von Braun. (Courtesy of the National Archives.)

A crowd gathers in a part of the stage subassembly area to watch the launch of a Saturn V on July 16, 1969. Behind the crowd, at rear left, are individual tanks for the S-I. The two televisions sprouting "rabbit ears" are sitting on wiring harness canisters for their viewing pleasure! (Courtesy of NASA.)

Sporting an appropriate white linen suite for the occasion, Mayor Victor H. Schiro addresses a crowd of Boeing Company employees during a "Splashdown Party" at the Municipal Auditorium in New Orleans on July 7, 1969. The mayor was often fond of saying, "If it's good for New Orleans, I'm for it." (Courtesy of the Victor Schiro Papers, Louisiana Collection, Tulane University.)

A white-coated technician inspects a newly arrived giant F-1 engine as it rests on its equally large transporter. (Courtesy of the New Orleans Public Library.)

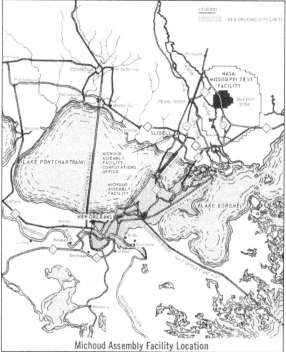

Michoud Assembly Facility Location

The location to static-test the boosters required an immense area that could contain not only the test stands, but a buffer zone as well, due to safety and noise considerations. The area would also be a site for spacecraft engineering and development facilities, and relatively accessible to other NASA field installations using ice-free, navigable waterways for year-round operations. (Courtesy of Mike Jetzer of heroicrelics.org.)

All boosters were static-tested and flight-certified at the Mississippi Test Facility (MTF), now the John C. Stennis Space Center in Hancock County, Mississippi. Persons outside the proscribed "buffer zone" of the MTF still talk about the rumble they heard and the ground vibrations they felt when the boosters were undergoing tests. A NASA report stated that "all first- and second-stage rockets of the Saturn V tested at the center performed their missions flawlessly." (Courtesy of NASA.)

A S-IC-9 booster, the first stage for an Apollo/Saturn V launch vehicle, undergoes static-test firing at the Mississippi Test Facility. Flame and smoke pour out of the deflector of the 407-foot-high test stand. The stand uses enough water in five minutes to supply a city of 10,000. The booster being tested is 138 feet high and produces 7.5 million pounds of thrust, equal to 160 million horsepower. (Author's collection.)

All water routes lead to Kennedy Space Center for the Saturn V booster rockets. The second stage was manufactured in Seal Beach, California. The McDonnell Douglas Astronautics Company of Huntington Beach, California, engineered and produced the third stage. Actual ground-test firings of the stages were performed at the Douglas Sacramento Test Center. The F-1 and J-2 engines are manufactured and tested at Rocketdyne in Canoga Park and Santa Susana, California. (Courtesy of Mike Jetzer of heroicrelics.org.)

NASA used five special barges for water transport: the *Poseidon* moved Saturn V first and second stages among Michoud, George C. Marshall Space Flight Center, and Cape Kennedy; the *Promise* carried the uprated Saturn I first stages between the three installations; *Palaemon* transported uprated Saturn I boosters between Michoud and Marshall; and the *Little Lake* and *Pearl River*, open-decked shuttle barges, moved Saturn V first and second stages from Michoud to the MTF. (Courtesy of Mike Jetzer of heroicrelics.org.)

The S-IC booster, built by The Boeing Company, was the first stage of the Saturn V. It sent the Apollo spacecraft on the first leg of manned lunar voyages. Here, an S-IC leaves Michoud for more tests and flight certification. (Courtesy of NASA.)

The size of Saturn rockets presented a unique set of transportation problems. Most of the stages were too large for conventional highway, rail, or air movement. The NASA barges *Poseidon*, *Promise*, and *Palaemon* worked the inland waterways and the open Gulf of Mexico into the Atlantic Ocean. The NASA barge *Orion* shuttled between the Huntington Beach and Sacramento, California, sites along the Pacific Coast. (Courtesy of the New Orleans Public Library.)

A "plastic suited" Saturn IB booster is loaded onto the NASA barge *Palaemon* for the river journey from Michoud Assembly Facility to NASA's George C. Marshall Space Flight Center in Huntsville, Alabama. The special plastic covering protected the booster during transport among assembly, testing, and launching facilities. (Courtesy of the National Archives.)

A Saturn V first-stage booster built by Boeing is carefully moved onto an awaiting barge at the Michoud slip. This slip was part of the improvements to the facility in the early 1960s. The slip area was extended and dredged to accommodate deepwater vessels. (Courtesy of the New Orleans Public Library.)

A Saturn SI-B booster is unloaded at George C. Marshall Space Flight Center in Hunstville, Alabama, from the covered barge *Poseidon*. The booster's trip originated at Michoud Assembly Facility in New Orleans. The barges are towed by tugboats during their 10-day river/ocean journeys from Huntsville to Kennedy Space Center in Cape Canaveral, Florida. (Courtesy of the National Archives.)

The circuitous route that all large space-launch vehicles endure is clearly drawn on this map of the southeastern United States. Navigable water access to all phases of booster fabrication and testing relative to the primary launch site was a fundamental concern. The route shown here was dubbed "the space crescent." (Courtesy of Mike Jetzer of heroicrelics.org.)

A NASA barge and tugboat round the crescent bend in the Mississippi River past Algiers Point, a neighborhood directly across the river from the French Quarter in New Orleans. The barge is making its way upriver to George C. Marshall Space Flight Center in Huntsville. The large expanse of buildings in the far background, along the riverbank, is the US Port of Embarkation and the entrance to the Inner Harbor Navigation Canal, or Industrial Canal. (Courtesy of NASA.)

The NASA barge and tugboat head upstream, passing under the Mississippi River Bridge on July 17, 1970. Just beyond the bridge is a dry dock on the left bank. Commercial shipping wharves and warehouses are on the right bank, beyond the photograph. The barge has just passed the foot of Canal Street, the central business district in New Orleans, on its way to Huntsville, Alabama. (Courtesy of NASA.)

A diverse group of personnel from all levels of the employment structure pose for one last photograph in June 1973, before the Saturn SI-B-8G leaves Building 103. (Courtesy of NASA.)

Employees gather in front of the Saturn SI-B-8G on its transporter as it makes its way to Michoud Slip and the barge that will take it to Cape Canaveral. (Courtesy of NASA.)

Dr. Wernher von Braun stands before a configuration of F-1 engines attached to a Saturn V booster rocket. Dr. von Braun exemplified what came to be known as the "von Braun Paradigm": the belief that humans are destined to physically explore the solar system, as he often described in *Collier's* magazine in the 1950s. For von Braun, humans were the most powerful and flexible exploration tool imaginable. (Author's collection.)

Members of the House of Representatives pose for a postcard photograph before they vote on a NASA authorization bill on May 23, 1973. Amid budgetary concerns, declining public interest, and a perceived détente between the United States and the Soviet Union, the US Congress voted to end funding for the Apollo program. (Author's collection.)

Four

SPACE TRANSPORTATION SYSTEM
THE SPACE SHUTTLE, 1973–2011

The space shuttle ushered in an era of sustained science and space exploration, as opposed to an international race to the moon. In 1972, George C. Marshall Space Flight Center designated Skylab, a completely American-built experimental space station, and the space shuttle to be its top priorities. The strategy called for the shuttle program to be in place after the last Saturn rocket launched Skylab.

By the late 1960s, NASA began plans for the maximum use of Apollo technology in broader programs that would engender more detailed scientific objectives. A Saturn V launched Skylab on May 14, 1973. Later, Saturn IB rockets launched three different three-man crews to the Skylab space station that demonstrated man's ability to withstand long periods of weightlessness and adaptability to the space environment. At the outset, Skylab was to remain in space long enough to be visited by the shuttle fleet, but high solar activity forced it to reenter Earth's atmosphere, disintegrating in the process, on July 1, 1979.

Pres. Richard M. Nixon proposed the reusable space-launch system in January 1972, and in July, the Martin-Marietta Co. (now Lockheed Martin Corp.) was awarded the contract to design, build, and produce the external tank component of the three-component system, which also included an orbiter and a pair of solid-rocket boosters. Together, they became a "truck," hauling satellites, experiments, and spare parts.

The external tank was to be a new, original design based on Saturn missile and aircraft technology concepts that would form the structural backbone of the shuttle launch system. However, it would be the only nonreusable component of the system, falling back to Earth, usually into the Indian Ocean, as the orbiter continued its ascent.

Predictably, a facility modification project began as the managers, engineers, and production specialists arrived in Michoud in 1973. Tool design and tooling began in 1974, while manufacturing began in 1975.

The shuttle program endured for 30 years, surviving accidents, hurricanes, budget increases, and cuts. Space shuttles carried over 100 primary payloads into orbit, including parts of the International Space Station.

From the outset, Dr. Wernher von Braun was an advocate of the imaginary arts as a way to both brainstorm details and depict yet-to-be-built space vehicles to the general public. (Courtesy of NASA.)

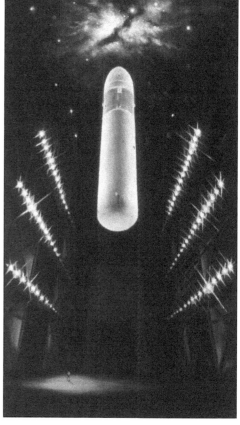

Much conceptual art was derived from rough drawings by engineers, such as this portrayal of an external tank as it leaves an ascendant space shuttle. These representations played an integral role in persuading top-level NASA officials to fund new projects. (Courtesy of NASA.)

The production floor of Building 103 undergoes minor alterations. Plant modifications continued into the 1980s to accommodate an evolving external tank design. (Courtesy of NASA.)

Martin-Marietta Co. (now Lockheed Martin Corp.) spent at least two years in the mid-1970s on design and partial fabrication of tools and plant modification before moving on to production. (Courtesy of NASA.)

Further strengthening of the production floor was accomplished by excavation of the floor, then driving down creosote-treated pilings. (Courtesy of NASA.)

A greatly strengthened foundation was an important part of Building 114, known as the "High Bay." Construction began in mid-1978 as part of the facility modification project. (Courtesy of NASA.)

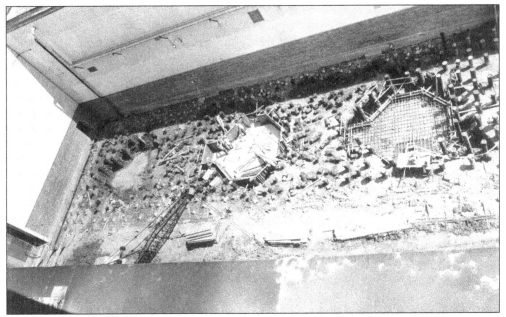

This photograph was taken from the roof of the Vertical Assembly Building (VAB). Shown here is the High Bay's network of foundation pilings and the formation of the "cells" that will support the hydrogen, intertank, and liquid oxygen tanks. These are the contents of the external tank. It is here that these components will undergo further processing after leaving the production floor of Building 103 (at the top portion of the photograph). (Courtesy of NASA.)

High Bay construction continues in September 1978 as the closely spaced, creosote-coated pilings are covered with reinforcing mesh and concrete. This process resulted in a highly reinforced floor area and the formation of the cells for various tank processes. (Courtesy of NASA.)

The High Bay was part of the new construction required for external tank production. It is conveniently located between the VAB (left) and Building 103, which houses the main production area. (Courtesy of NASA.)

A technician calibrates a Gemcore riveter as it attaches stringers to panels, or the skin, of the intertank to make it stiffer. The machine drills a hole between the two pieces, inserts a rivet, and squeezes the rivet into place. (Courtesy of NASA.)

The black truss and the cylinder form the assembly of the LH2 tank-proof test fixture. This assembly would be mounted onto two big trusses anchored into the ground in Building 451. Each LH2 tank would be tested to simulate flight-load levels. The proof test verified the adequacy of the welds before the tank was sprayed with foam insulation and mated to the intertank and LO2 tank. (Courtesy of NASA.)

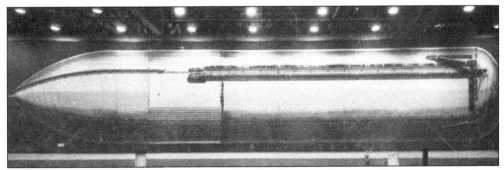

In 1975, Martin-Marietta Co. sent holiday greetings with this Christmas card design to its employees at Michoud, assuring them that important contract milestones had been met, thereby expediting the move to production. Also, employees and their families were thanked for their long hours of work and their dedicated efforts. (Author's collection.)

Engineers, managers, and directors stand before a painting on canvas that hung in Building 103. The image served as a life-sized reminder of their mission in the space program. (Courtesy of NASA.)

Using methods pioneered by Dr. Wernher von Braun, a full-scale conceptual painting on canvas of the space shuttle's external tank was used to convey to the public via news and print media the scale and importance of this component of the shuttle system. (Courtesy of NASA.)

Joseph Winkler, an associate engineer (left), and a group of employees take time out for a photograph. (Courtesy of NASA.)

A small group of engineers stands before tool No. 5019 major weld, used to weld the tank domes to barrel sections. (Courtesy of NASA.)

NASA attracted engineering talent from all over the world. By the mid-1970s, Michoud experienced a "British Invasion" of engineers. Members of the Stress Analysis Group–Hydrogen Tank are, from left to right, an unidentified stress analyst from Great Britain, Vic Boyd (Wales), Ron Rae (Scotland), Fulvio Manto (Italy), and an unidentified stress analyst from Great Britain. The unidentified chap seated in the background was also from Great Britain. (Author's collection.)

Stress analyst Fulvio Manto takes time out from thinking at his desk in the east wing of Building 102. In the background is a now-extinct drafting table/machine. It has since been replaced by Computer Aided Design (CAD). (Author's collection.)

The aft end of the ET LH2 tank rests on the circular welding fixture, used to assemble the LH2 tank by welding each successive barrel assembly, with associated circular frame, and ending with the forward dome assembly. Visible inside are the LH2 feed line and the anti-vortex baffle assembly (four vanes). The baffles prevented the vortex generated by the draining of the liquid hydrogen as the shuttle climbed toward orbit. (Courtesy of NASA.)

One of the first external tanks is rolled into the High Bay. Behind it stands the Vertical Assembly Building. (Courtesy of NASA.)

An early external tank without its nose cone is hoisted into a bay in the VAB. (Courtesy of NASA.)

An external tank is lifted off its transporter and into a cell for further cleaning of its interior tanks and completion of foam applications. (Courtesy of NASA.)

LIQUID HYDROGEN TRIM & WELD FIXTURE
(Foreground) AND LIQUID OXYGEN TRIM
& WELD FIXTURE   1/20/77

On January 20, 1977, a liquid hydrogen trim and weld fixture (center) and a liquid oxygen trim and weld fixture (right) rest on their own tool No. 5019 major weld. (Courtesy of NASA.)

An early external tank is gently loaded onto a barge for its next stop at a NASA field installation. (Courtesy of NASA.)

The Main Propulsion Test Article (MPTA), the first tank built, arrives at the Mississippi Test Facility (MTF, now John C. Stennis Space Center) for a static propulsion test. The open-decked NASA barges *Little Lake* and *Pearl River* shuttled the tanks between Michoud and MTF. Test stands A-1 and A-2 conducted the static tests. Both are US National Historic Landmarks and listed in the National Register of Historic Places. (Courtesy of NASA.)

It took two tugboats to maneuver a NASA barge carrying one of three early test-article tanks through the inland waterways between Michoud and MTF, a distance of approximately 40 miles. (Courtesy of NASA.)

The MPTA is hoisted from the barge to the test stand, where it is positioned and secured. A shuttle simulator system, duplicating a real shuttle stack, is achieved by mounting three engines on the test article, but without the solid rocket boosters (SRBs). The MPTA tank is then filled for the commencement of the static propulsion test, which simulates the flow of liquid hydrogen and liquid oxygen. (Courtesy of NASA.)

The detail fabrication crew takes time out for a photograph in front of the first external tank produced at Michoud. This tank was known simply as the Main Propulsion Test Article. (Courtesy of NASA.)

One of three test article tanks rolls out at Michoud to great acclaim. Prime contractor Martin-Marietta Co. built three test articles for specific purposes: Main Propulsion Test Article, Structural Test Article, and Ground Vibration Test Article. During the Apollo program, boosters known as "Battleships" were made specifically for test purposes. (Courtesy of NASA.)

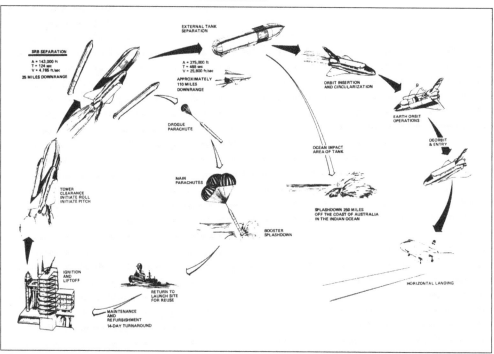

This graphic depicts the launch and return to Earth of the Space Transportation System, both of which took place at Kennedy Space Center at Cape Canaveral, Florida. This was the first space vehicle to accomplish this feat. A launch is possible from both California and Florida, but a launch from Florida to the east allows the craft to follow the rotation of the Earth and stay relatively close to the equator, giving it a speed boost in orbit. (Courtesy of NASA.)

The first external tank, known as the Main Propulsion Test Article (MPTA), rolled out of Building 103 on September 9, 1977. It was used in the first static firing of the three main engines at the Mississippi Test Facility. Martin-Marietta Co., the prime contractor, designed and assembled the external tanks at Michoud. (Courtesy of NASA.)

After the first two operational test flights in 1981, NASA was awarded the Robert J. Collier Trophy "for the greatest achievement in aeronautics or astronautics in America." The 525-pound trophy is awarded annually and is on permanent display at the National Air and Space Museum in Washington, DC. Robert Collier, an aviator and humanitarian, published *Collier's Weekly*, a magazine to which Dr. Wernher von Braun was a frequent contributor. (Courtesy of NASA.)

The sixth space shuttle external tank, and the last one built to initial design specifications, rolls onto the NASA barge *Orion* for a five-day trip to Kennedy Space Center in Florida. Due to modifications regarding materials, after this first-version standard weight model, future tanks would weigh 6,000 pounds less, enabling the orbiter to carry heavier payloads. (Author's collection.)

The production area of Building 103 contains several external tanks in various states of assembly in 1982. After the successful operational test flights in 1981, the impetus for regular flights into space had been established. (Author's collection.)

Shown here are two second-version lightweight external tanks in production in Building 103. (Courtesy of NASA.)

Technicians with Martin-Marietta Co. conduct optical inspections on two of the three external tanks in production. Note the size of the tanks relative to the technicians. (Courtesy of NASA.)

Bernie White, an employee of Martin-Marietta Co., built and maintained an expansive model of the entire Michoud Assembly Facility. Here, tour groups are ushered into the model room for an introduction to the vast facility after a brief walk along the perimeter of the production area. (Courtesy of NASA.)

The three components of the space shuttle system are clearly visible here: the orbiter *Atlantis*, two SRBs, and the external tank. This shuttle awaits launch at Kennedy Space Center on September 16, 1996. STS-79 flew a 10-day mission, during which it docked with the Mir Space Station. (Courtesy of NASA.)

The MPTA rests on its transporter in front of the Vehicle Assembly Building. For the first two missions, STS-1 and STS-2, the tanks were covered with a white latex paint that was believed to protect its insulating foam from the sun's ultraviolet rays while on the launch pad. Eliminating the nonessential paint freed up 600 pounds for additional payload. (Courtesy of NASA.)

NASA frequently recognized the contributions made by the employees of its prime contractors. Here, astronaut Mike Lounge (right) presents the Astronauts Personal Achievement Award to director of engineering Jon Dutton on October 26, 1988. Dutton originated a configuration within the hydrogen tank barrel panels that reduced stress on the welds, creating a more robust piece of hardware, known as "The Dutton Groove." (Courtesy of Mary Ann Dutton.)

The MPTA, sporting a coat of "protective" white latex paint, is maneuvered into Building 103 for further inspections. (Courtesy of NASA.)

A large contingent of employees of Martin-Marietta Manned Space Systems gathers before the largest assembly of external tanks under one roof at Michoud. (Courtesy of NASA.)

Spectators watch a static test firing of an external tank at John C. Stennis Space Center in 2009. After several minutes, the massive clouds of vapor create an artificial rainfall, usually falling onto the spectators. A large tent is provided to ward off the often-blistering sun and the artificial rainfall. (Courtesy of NASA.)

An external tank, without a layer of white latex paint and newly arrived from Michoud, is hoisted onto a test stand at John C. Stennis Space Center. The tank's Thermo-Protection System (TPS) acts like a vacuum bottle to protect the propellants inside from reacting to changes produced by frictional forces in the air outside. (Courtesy of NASA.)

External tank 133 rolls off the NASA *Pegasus* barge at Kennedy Space Center in Florida. It powered the STS-129 mission to the International Space Station in November 2009. (Courtesy of NASA.)

Lockheed Martin's fuel tank ET-129 enters a NASA barge. External tank number designations followed a consecutive numbering system. Space shuttle missions (STS) were labeled based on a shuttle manifest that assigned numbers based on type of payload and possible changes in the manifest and/or payload at any given time. (Courtesy of NASA.)

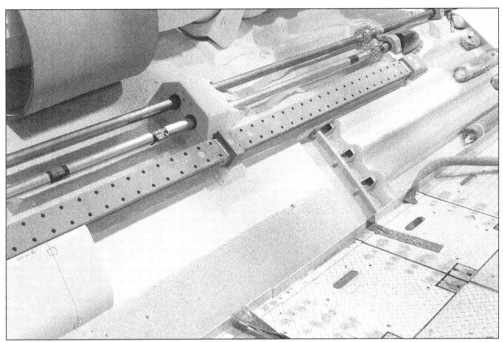

The Protuberance Air Load Ramp, better known as the PAL, was one of the focus areas for the external tank "Return to Flight" program after the February 1, 2003, *Columbia* accident. (Courtesy of NASA.)

The 121st external tank (ET-121) rolls out of Building 103 on its way to Cape Canaveral for launch. (Courtesy of NASA.)

The crew of STS-114, the "Return to Flight" after the 2003 *Columbia* accident, poses during a visit to Michoud. ET-120, shown here, will power them into orbit. Pictured here are, left to right, mission specialist Charles Camarda, pilot James Kelly, mission specialist Soichi Noguchi, mission specialist Wendy Lawrence, mission specialist Stephen Robinson, Comdr. Eileen Collins, and mission specialist Andrew Thomas. (Courtesy of NASA.)

STS-114 commander Eileen Collins listens intently as a technician explains the work being done on an external tank's intertank flange area during production. (Courtesy of NASA.)

Astronauts, either individually or a mission's entire crew, were frequent visitors to Michoud during the space shuttle era. The crew of STS-121, pictured here with ET-119 at Michoud, are, from left to right, pilot Mark Kelly, Comdr. Steve Lindsey, and mission specialists Lisa Nowak, Piers Sellers, Stephanie Wilson, and Mike Fossum. (Courtesy of NASA.)

External tank ET-128 is on its way to a NASA barge docked at Michoud Slip. It will then travel to Kennedy Space Center on Florida's east coast. During the five-day sea journey, ET-128 will traverse the Intercoastal Canal to the Gulf of Mexico, around the Florida peninsula into the Atlantic Ocean, and then into the Banana River at Cape Canaveral. (Courtesy of NASA.)

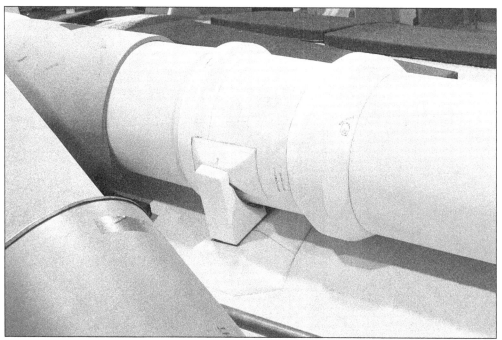

The liquid oxygen feedline bellows was a focus on the external tank prior to "Return to Flight." A large feedline runs from the liquid oxygen tank, located at the top of the external tank, to an umbilical at the bottom of the tank, connecting it to the orbiter. As the ET expands and contracts during tanking and inflight, the feedline bellows, or expansion joints, allow for movement without undue stress. (Courtesy of NASA.)

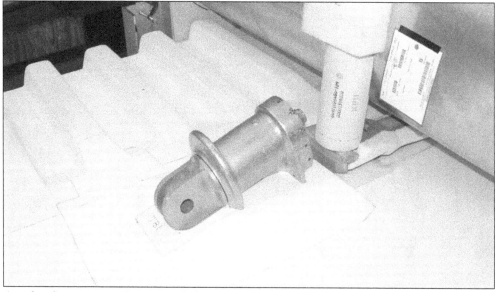

Another focus prior to "Return to Flight" was the forward bipod fitting, previously part of a bipod foam ramp. It was redesigned to minimize potential debris by eliminating the large insulating foam bipod ramps by adding four-rod heaters below each fitting in a new copper plate. Structural testing performed at Michoud demonstrated the load capability of the redesigned fitting to withstand external forces acting on the structure. (Courtesy of NASA.)

The ET's bipod area is being readied to receive the redesigned bipod fitting. The four-rod heaters (right) have been moved to expose the new copper plate. The copper plate with heaters is sandwiched between the bipod fitting and the existing phenolic thermal isolating pad. The thermal isolator pad helps reduce heat loss from the copper plate into the extremely cold liquid hydrogen tank. (Courtesy of NASA.)

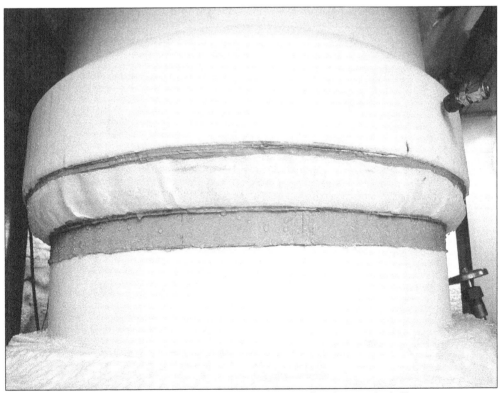

The redesigned liquid oxygen feedline bellows has a foam "drip lip" on the bellows cover, or rain shield. The bellows cover is squared at the bottom and has a slight, 10-degree angle. This allows condensation to run off, reducing the potential for ice buildup, particularly on a hot and humid day in Florida. (Courtesy of NASA.)

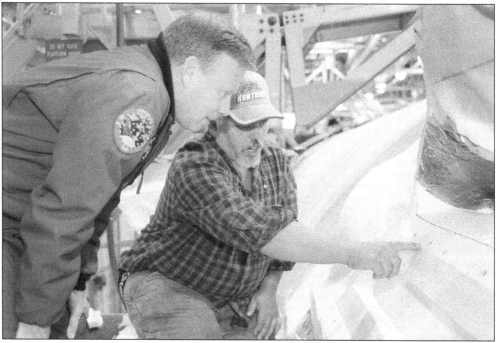

Comdr. Steve Lindsey of STS-133 listens as a technician with Lockheed Martin Corp. points out details of external tank ET-138, which powered the orbiter *Discovery* to the final scheduled shuttle mission to the International Space Station, on February 24, 2011. (Courtesy of NASA.)

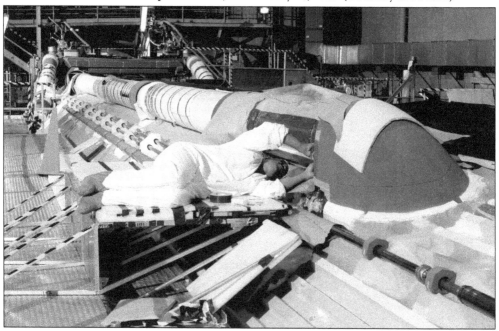

A Lockheed Martin Corp. technician installs a liquid oxygen tank feedline bellows heater on an external tank. The feedline carries liquid oxygen from the tank to the main engines. The bellows are the joints that allow the feedline to move, or flex, when the tank is assembled, fueled, during liftoff, and during ascent. (Courtesy of NASA.)

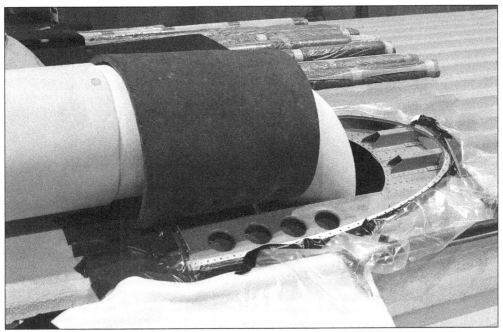

The external tank's in-flight imaging system is seen here attached to ET-120 at Michoud. (Courtesy of NASA.)

The Protuberance Air Load Ramp, or PAL, is shown on ET-120 without its foam covering. (Courtesy of NASA.)

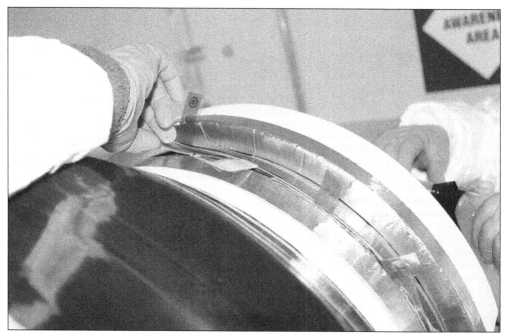

This copper-nickel alloy metal strip heater, being applied to the topmost bellows of an external tank's liquid oxygen feedline, is designed to keep the bellows area slightly warmer than freezing, about 40 degrees Fahrenheit. This reduces the amount of ice and frost formed prior to launch. (Courtesy of NASA.)

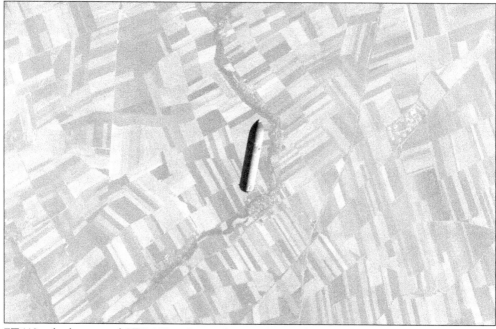

ET-118, which powered STS-115 in September 2006, was photographed by astronauts on board, 21 minutes into their ascent into orbit. The external tank falls in a preplanned trajectory 8.5 minutes after launch. Most of the tank disintegrates in the atmosphere, and the rest falls into the Indian Ocean. (Courtesy of NASA.)

The 38 members of Lockheed Martin Manned Space Systems Ride-Out Crew stand before a minimally damaged external tank ET-122. The crew received NASA's Exceptional Bravery Medal. Congressman Charlie Melancon of Louisiana's Third Congressional District sponsored House Resolution 892 to recognize the crew's ability to "save Michoud, the External Tanks, and other hardware and allow the resumption of production operations five weeks after Hurricane Katrina struck on August 29, 2005." (Courtesy of NASA.)

The crew of STS-116 gathers at the 225-foot level of Launch Pad 39B at Kennedy Space Center. The massiveness of the external tank relative to the reusable solid rocket boosters is clearly seen. The crew members are, from left to right, Comdr. Mark Polansky, pilot Bill Oefelein, and mission specialists Nicholas Patrick, Robert Curbeam, Thomas Reiter of the European Space Agency, Joan Higginbotham, and Sunita Williams. (Author's collection.)

A solitary forward section of an external tank occupies a relatively small space in the production area of Building 103 as Lockheed Martin employees head outside for the rollout of the last external tank to be used for a space shuttle mission. (Courtesy of Fulvio Manto.)

After rolling out of Building 420, at final assembly checkout, ET-138 rests on its transporter for all to see. The tank awaits its one-mile trip to the Michoud Slip and then on to Kennedy Space Center in Cape Canaveral, Florida. (Courtesy of Fulvio Manto.)

Astronaut Barry "Butch" Wilmore, who piloted STS-129 and served as Spacecraft Communicator (CAPCOM) for STS-135, speaks to a Lockheed Martin employee while astronaut Mark E. Kelly (right background) looks on at the festivities. They are taking shelter under a tent on a very hot and humid day in southeastern Louisiana. ET-138 (background) powered STS-134 on its last mission, of which Kelly was the commander. (Courtesy of Fulvio Manto.)

Seen here at center is Congressman Anh Joseph Quang Cao, Republican representative of the Second Congressional District, where Michoud is located. He is standing before ET-138 with several of his constituents. They are, from left to right, Chinh Hoang, Business Operations; Hailey Vu, Information Technology; Chau Luong, software specialist; Son Van Chu, System Control; an unidentified Lockheed Martin employee; and Thanh Tran, Information Technology. (Courtesy of Fulvio Manto.)

Lockheed Martin Manned Space System employees get ready for their "second line" accompaniment (note the decorated umbrella on the right) for ET-134 to meet its NASA barge. Chris Bourgeois, Production Management and Technical Operations (right), poses with an unidentified Lockheed Martin employee. In the background at right wearing sunglasses is Debra J. Berkman, Performance Enhancement Office. (Courtesy of Fulvio Manto.)

The refreshment and shade tent also served as the gathering area for employees for the second line parade. (Courtesy of Fulvio Manto.)

Lockheed Martin employees are armed with hats, cameras, umbrellas, feathered fans, and commemorative T-shirts and handkerchiefs (to facilitate the second line). They are accompanied by the Storyville Stompers Brass Band. This is the beginning of the one-mile parade to deliver the last external tank produced at Michoud. (Courtesy of Fulvio Manto.)

Commemorative T-shirts sporting the tagline "Finish Strong" were the order of the day for the event. Mark E. Javery (left) of Program Management and Technical Operations at Michoud, and Neil Otte (right), NASA's chief engineer for the External Tank Project at George C. Marshall Space Flight Center at Huntsville, Alabama, look on as the festivities continue. (Courtesy of Fulvio Manto.)

As the handkerchief says, "make the last tank the 'best tank.'" Lockheed Martin commemorated 37 years of 135 successful tank deliveries to NASA during 25 years of the space shuttle. The crew of STS-134 included Comdr. Mark E. Kelly, pilot Greg H. Johnson, and mission specialists Michael Fincke, Greg Chamitoff, Andrew Feustel, and the European Space Agency's Roberto Vittori of Italy. ET-138 powered STS-134 into orbit. (Courtesy of Mary Ann Dutton.)

Five

BACK TO THE FUTURE
AT MAF

As NASA transitions into new endeavors, Michoud Assembly Facility (MAF) has evolved into a diverse, multi-tenant community. Current occupants of the versatile site include the US Department of Agriculture, the US Department of the Interior, the US Coast Guard, the National Center for Advanced Manufacturing (NCAM), Blade Dynamics, B-K Manufacturing, British Petroleum, The Boeing Company, Lockheed Martin Corp., and Big Easy Studios, LLC, a film production company.

Lockheed Martin Corp. is the prime contractor for the Orion Multi-Purpose Crew Vehicle, designed for human-rated, deep-space exploration, including to asteroids, the moon, and Mars. The vehicle will carry a crew of up to six astronauts and provide a safe abort during all mission phases. At Michoud, Lockheed Martin is also building part of the proof-of-concept lifting body for Sierra Nevada Corporation's Dream Chaser, a low-Earth orbiter designed to service the International Space Station. Whereas the space shuttle was described as a "truck" for space, the Dream Chaser is characterized as a suburban utility vehicle, or SUV, for space. The vehicle will be powered into orbit atop an Atlas V rocket, whose design originated in the 1950s.

The Boeing Company returns to its roots at MAF as the prime contractor for NASA's Space Launch System, an advanced heavy-lift launch vehicle designed to travel beyond low-Earth orbit but remain flexible for a variety of crew and cargo missions. Upon completion, the Space Launch System's core stage will be approximately 212 feet tall with a diameter of 27.6 feet. The stage will carry cryogenic liquid hydrogen and liquid oxygen to fuel its four RS-25 engines. This engine, designed for the main engines on the space shuttle, are being built by Aerojet Rocketdyne of Sacramento, California. Each RS-25 engine will provide 512,000 pounds of thrust.

The avionics and computers, which will be housed in the core stage of the Space Launch System, are also being built by The Boeing Company. Space Launch System's first flight test, carrying an unmanned Orion Multi-Purpose Crew Vehicle, is scheduled for 2017.

As the US space program charts its course through the 21st century, potential "heroic relics" continue to be manufactured at Michoud Assembly Facility.

This single blade, used in wind turbines, was fabricated at MAF. It is en route to an energy-generating wind farm. A Saturn V booster rocket is on display in the background. Blade Dynamics is a UK manufacturer of advanced wind-turbine rotors and one of the relatively new occupants at MAF since 2009. (Courtesy of NASA.)

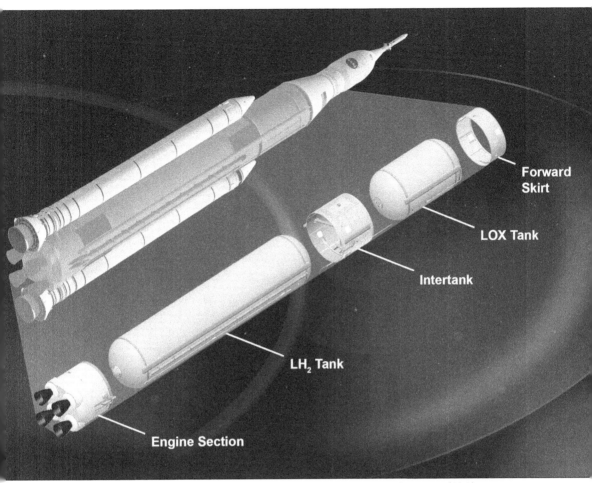

This schematic diagram shows the components of NASA's Space Launch System (SLS) core stage, currently under construction at MAF by The Boeing Company. (Courtesy of NASA.)

The MAF machine shop floor in Building 103 is seen here as it tools up for SLS manufacture and assembly. (Courtesy of NASA.)

The floor of the Vehicle Assembly Building is being modified once more, with concrete and rebar, to provide a steady foundation for tests that require a high degree of precision. When the test subject is big and long, it is imperative that it remain immobile for accurate test readings. Errors involving inches off the target number during a test are not an option; the goal is to achieve the smallest of tolerances possible. (Courtesy of NASA.)

An on-site, mid-size autoclave is used to cure components made from advanced composites material. (Courtesy of NASA.)

A universal friction-stir welding machine displays its turntable, used to hold the item to be welded. The welding is achieved in all directions with a rotating head and with all degrees of freedom: up, down, in, and out. The process is done without a welding rod or flame. Instead, two pieces of material are joined by bringing them close enough to plasticize the material without liquefying it. These welding machines are part of the National Center for Advanced Manufacturing at MAF. (Courtesy of NASA.)

A crane with spreader bars carefully moves a propellant tank barrel for the SLS in the newly constructed Vertical Assembly Building constructed for NASA's new venture. (Courtesy of NASA.)

Despite the development of very precise machinery, nothing can replace the use of optical alignment. Here, a propellant tank barrel for the Space Launch System is carefully lowered onto its supports in the VAB. (Courtesy of NASA.)

An engineer adjusts a fiber-placing machine head, used to make advanced composite components, some of which may require curing in an autoclave. (Courtesy of NASA.)

NASA administrator Charles F. Bolden Jr. (center), a retired US Marine Corps major general and former astronaut, is given a tour of MAF accompanied by Michoud Assembly Facility director Roy Malone (left) and Space Launch System program manager Todd May (right). NASA's emergency preparedness officer at MAF, Stephen A. Turner (far left, rear), secures a safe, smooth visit for everyone. (Courtesy of NASA.)

The Space Launch System's crew capsule, being built by Lockheed Martin, returns to Earth in this realistic artist's rendering. (Courtesy of NASA.)

Technicians work to adapt an existing Century-Detroit machine tool for use in friction-stir welding, an essential method used in the construction of the Space Launch System currently under way. (Courtesy of NASA.)

Boeing fabrication specialists Todd Duhon (left) and Guillermo Ladut consult on the calibration of the Gore Weld tool to be used to build the SLS's rocket cryogenic stage. (Courtesy of NASA.)

Several friction-stir welding machines were originally designed to build the upper stages of the Ares I and Ares IV, but these programs have been cancelled. In addition, the welding machines are too small for the Space Launch System's requirements. They remain on the production floor. Note the dome welding fixture in the foreground. (Courtesy of NASA.)

A dome, part of the propellant tank being built by The Boeing Company, rests on the turntable of a friction-stir welding machine. (Courtesy of NASA.)

A crew module structure of the Orion Multi-Purpose Crew Vehicle (MPCV) is shown being moved by a lifting fixture to the next position in the production process. (Courtesy of NASA.)

A crew module structure of the Orion MPCV is readied for Exploration Flight Test No. 1, otherwise known as EFT1. (Courtesy of NASA.)

Shown here is Lockheed Martin's aft assembly of a crew module structure for the Orion MPCV. (Courtesy of NASA.)

Exploration Flight Test No. 1 structure, or EFT1, built by the Lockheed Martin Corp., is lifted and moved to the next position in the production process. (Courtesy of NASA.)

EFT1 is readied for shipping as technicians prepare the platform on which it sits and materials around it for protection. The large air duct provides fresh air to technicians working inside the EFT1 during this process. (Courtesy of NASA.)

A full-scale model of Sierra Nevada Corporation's Dream Chaser is seen here at its headquarters in Sparks, Nevada. The Lockheed Martin Corp. is currently one of three bidders to construct the frame for this Orbital Flight Vehicle. Employing the capabilities of the National Center for Advanced Manufacturing, Lockheed Martin is proposing the use of composite materials, no metals or welding, for the frame, to be built at MAF. Completion will take place at its facility in Fort Worth, Texas. (Courtesy of Sierra Nevada Corporation.)

An artist's rendering depicts a Dream Chaser Orbital Flight Vehicle atop an Atlas V rocket on the launch pad, ready for low-Earth orbit. Currently, human-rated Atlas V rockets, originally designed in the 1950s by the Convair Division of General Dynamics Corporation, are produced by a joint venture of Lockheed Martin and Boeing under the aegis of United Launch Alliance. (Courtesy of Sierra Nevada Corporation.)

The Dream Chaser, a type of "lifting body," will travel to the International Space Station in low-Earth orbit and return to Earth via any runway available. Fabrication of composite structures began in January 2014, with cabin ring frame production taking place in the same location as the epic programs before it—Michoud Assembly Facility. (Courtesy of Sierra Nevada Corporation.)

Visit us at
arcadiapublishing.com